Mine Mine Mine

Said The

Porcupine

By Alex English

Illustrated by Emma Levey

A porcupine popped into Alfie's today.

"Howdy," said Alfie,

"would you like to play?"

"How about making a spaceship from stuff?"

"MINE!"

said the porcupine,

"Keep your paws off."

"We could play...

...football

...or robots

...or planes."

"Or paint a huge dinosaur covered in spines."

But the porcupine said, "MINE!"

"MINE!"

"Fine!" said Alfie.
"I won't play with you."

"I'll play on my own
in the land of Kaboo."

The porcupine played with
the robot and drum but the
land of Kaboo seemed to be
much more fun.

Alfie **jumped** and **galumphed** and he ran and he **skied**.

He **sang** as he **swang** through imaginary trees.

"Can I play there too?"
asked the porcupine.

"PLEASE?"

"Of course," said Alfie, "just hold my hand."

And they danced and they pranced through his make-believe land.

Alfie said, "Now you can be my best friend."

Mine Mine Mine said the Porcupine

An original concept by author Alex English

© Alex English

Illustrated by Emma Levey

MAVERICK ARTS PUBLISHING LTD

Studio 3A, City Business Centre, 6 Brighton Road, Horsham, West Sussex, RH13 5BB

© Maverick Arts Publishing Limited October 2016 +44 (0)1403 256941

A CIP catalogue record for this book is available at the British Library.

ISBN 978-1-84886-217-3

Maverick

arts publishing

www.maverickbooks.co.uk